HEROES, LOVERS,

and Others

The Story of Latinos in Hollywood

CLARA E. RODRÍGUEZ

Smithsonian Books • Washington

Copy editor: Katherine Kimball
Production editor: Robert A. Poarch
Designer: Janice Wheeler

Library of Congress Cataloging-in-Publication data
Rodríguez Clara E., 1944–
    Heroes, lovers, and others : the story of Latinos in
    Hollywood / Clara E. Rodríguez.
        p.   cm.
    Includes bibliographical references and index.
    ISBN 1-58834-111-9 (alk. Paper)
    1. Hispanic American motion picture actors and actresses—Biography.
2. Hispanic Americans in the motion picture industry—Biography. 3. Hispanic
Americans in motion pictures. 4. Latin Americans in motion pictures. I. Title.

    PN1995.9.H47 R63 2004
    791.43'652968—dc22   2003055623

British Library Cataloguing-in-Publication Data is available

Manufactured in the United States of America
10 09 08 07 06 05 04   5 4 3 2 1

♾ The paper used in this publication meets the minimum requirements of the
American National Standard for Information Sciences—Permanence of Paper
for Printed Library Materials ANSI Z39.48—1992.

For permission to reproduce the photographs appearing in this book, please
correspond directly with the owners of the works, as listed in the individual
captions. Smithsonian Books does not retain reproduction rights for these
photographs or illustrations individually, or maintain a file of addresses for
photo sources.

Photo credits: page 8, 9, courtesy Smithsonian Institution, National Museum
of American History, Archives Center, Baden Collection; 11, 14, 13, 16, 18, 20, 21,
45, 67, courtesy Smithsonian Institution Libraries; 33, 50, 55, 60, 63, 67, 76, 77,
84, 86, 87, 89, 92, 96, 113, 115, 117, 120, 123, 132, 136, 183, courtesy The Museum of
Modern Art Film Stills Archive; 36, courtesy of the Academy of Motion Picture
Arts and Sciences; 39, courtesy Billy Rose Theatre Collection, The New York
Public Library for the Performing Arts, Astor, Lenox, and Tilden Foundations;
126, 139, 169, 201, 207, 209, 215, 218, 222, 225, 229, 231, 232, 234, 235, 238, 241,
courtesy Photofest; 129, courtesy Mrs. Paul Jarrico; 141, 143, courtesy the Felipe
N. Torres Papers, Centro de Estudios Puertorriqueños, Hunter College, City
University of New York; 171, 175, 202, 210, courtesy the Academy of Motion
Picture Arts and Sciences; 173, courtesy Cheech Marin; 177, courtesy Hector
Elizondo; 203, Teitelbaum Artists Group; 205, courtesy Antonio Banderas.

Contents

Preface

Some film stars have been shooting stars—they shine
and die out. Others grow and continue to flicker in the
sky—they become eternal legends. Still others were legends in their time but have since been forgotten. The
history of Latino film stars is filled with such stories.

One purpose of this book is to uncover the buried
history of Latino film stars in Hollywood films.
Another is to represent and reflect what the Smithsonian Institution has called "the changing American
kaleidoscope" ("Latino Oversight Committee, Smithsonian Announce Results of Study," press release,
October 15, 1997, 1). In this respect, the book seeks to
build a new awareness of Latino culture and history as
part of the full range of diversity in the United States.
I seek to give voice to those whom history has too often
ignored. I see my book as contributing to a shared
vision in which the remarkable range of human expe-
rience is understood through the histories of all
groups—in particular, those whose histories have not
received sufficient attention in the past.

The history of Latinos in film is a complex one, showing change over time as well as constants. The book is organized chronologically and thematically. The first chapter is a descriptive chapter that examines the earliest period of Latin film history. It establishes an important point of departure to which subsequent periods refer. The remaining chapters examine the primary stars and films in each of the five major eras of Latino film history. Chapter 2 focuses on the stars in the earliest periods of film, from 1910 to the 1930s. Chapter 3 examines the period surrounding World War II. The next three chapters examine, respectively, the cold war era, the modern era, and the postmodern era. This chronological focus on the films and film stars in each era explores how both the public personas and the film roles of Latino stars were influenced by the temper of the times and how the stars personally navigated their own sense of identity in these times.

A Few Words of Clarification

Many of the names of the actors discussed in this book have accents in their native language. For example, the names of Lupe Vélez and Dolores Del Río are both accented in Spanish. During their careers, however, these accents were generally ignored in English-language materials or on theater marquees. In later periods, accents and other diacritical marks were rarely used. More recently, film stars have begun to use accents. However, their use has not been (and is not) consistent. Therefore, with all due respect to those who prefer to retain accents in their names—and this includes myself—I have omitted most accents in this text.

Many terms are used today to denote those of Spanish-speaking heritage—Hispanic, Spanish, Latino, Spanish American, Latino American, and American Latino—and many arguments have been advanced for the use of particular terms. In this book I tend to use the words "Latino" and "Hispanic" somewhat interchangeably. Notwithstanding, I use the word "Latin" as well, because that was the term most in vogue in the early part of film history. It is still used by many in the media today, as in "a new Latin actress" or "Latin music." I also use "Chicano" to refer to people of Mexican origin who have been born or raised in the United States. The term came into vogue during the late 1960s and early 1970s, and it reflects a political consciousness borne of the Chicano student movement. Although it is often a generational marker for many who came of age during those decades, the terms "Chicano" and "Chicana" have also been embraced by elders and children who share in the political ideals of the movement. In the past, the term was associated with those who identified themselves as nationalists and rejected accommodation strategies, but today it is much more about social justice and political and community empowerment (Vicki Ruiz, personal correspondence, September 30, 2003).

This book does not intend to be encyclopedic; rather, it presents an overview within a historical context. Consequently, many talented Latinos, both actors and those behind the cameras, are missing. I refer the reader to the selected readings listed at the end of this book, particularly two excellent and comprehensive works: Luis Reyes and Peter Rubie's 1994 *Hispanics in Hollywood: An Encyclopedia of Film and Television,* as well as their revised 2000 edition, *Hispanics in Hollywood: A Celebration of 100 Years in Film and Television;* and Gary D. Keller's *Biographical Handbook of Hispanics and United States Film* (1997).

Finally, great pains have been taken to ensure the accuracy of the material in this volume. However, a number of difficulties are inherent in research in this area—or, for that matter, in any area in which media images are often carefully constructed and protected. The age of actors (particularly in the earlier periods) may have been altered by the actors themselves or by their studios because of the concern with preserving youthful public images. Film dates may vary at times because they can refer to the date of completion, or first screening, or general release, or release in a new market. When there has been conflicting information on titles and release dates, I have followed the Internet Movie Database (www.imdb.com), the most popular source for this type of information. (For a fuller discussion of such issues in the realm of Latinos and film, see pages vii–ix in the introduction to the Keller volume cited above).

The Latino Kettle

This book focuses on Latinos as one group because this has been the dominant way they have been viewed by U.S. motion picture audiences, as Latins, Latinos, Hispanics, or just "Spanish," with occasional distinctions made by national origin. However, the Latino population is actually made up of a variety of groups that differ not only in terms of national histories, particular cultural cuisine, and the relations between their homeland and the United States, for example, but also in terms of general class status within the United States. Some of these differences are the result of particular migration histories. For example, the Cuban community's socioeconomic profile was skewed upward as a result of the early post-Castro migration of the 1960s, which brought political refugees who were generally skilled and from the upper-income classes in Cuba. In contrast, the labor migrations of Mexicans and Puerto Ricans after World War II contributed more members to the working class.

The perceived differences between the groups in this country are not necessarily reflective of their countries of origin. The higher status and stronger Republican bent of Cubans in the United States contrasts sharply with the political orientation and level of economic development in Cuba today. The differences are a function of who left, and why. As Celia Cruz, the late and great Cuban salsa singer, often said, "We [Latinos] are all brothers in a different country." We are all Latinos in the United States. However, even though many may identify in this way, most Latinos also hold on to their national-origin identities as Puerto Rican, Mexican, and so on.

How large is each of the groups in the United States?

According to the U.S. census, Mexicans comprised the majority of all Latinos (58.5 percent, or 20.6 million) in 2000. The 3.4 million Puerto Ricans were the second-largest group, constituting 9.6 percent of all Latinos in the United States. If the 3.8 million Puerto Ricans residing in Puerto Rico are included, this percentage more than doubles (to 20.4 percent). Cubans were the next-largest single national-origin group, with 3.5 percent, followed by Dominicans, with 2.2 percent. The Central American countries collectively accounted for 4.8 percent of the total Latino pie, with Salvadorans (at 1.9 percent) and Guatemalans (at 1.1 percent) being the two largest groups among them. South Americans constituted another 3.8 percent of the total U.S. Latino population, with Colombians (at 1.3 percent) the largest group. All the other countries in Central and South America constituted less than 1 percent each of the total Latino population.

One of the most interesting results of the 2000 census is the large proportion of people who said they were Hispanic or Latino but did not give a national origin (17.3 percent). Some of these may have parents from more than one country, others may be fourth- or fifth-generation "Latino Americans" who no longer identify with any particular Latin American country. It is this group that has shown the greatest growth over time. It may be that, with more time residing in the United States, common experiences, intermarriage, and the tendency to see all Latinos as the same, there is increasing use of pan-Latino terms and greater bonding among all groups.

At present, however, there is still a very diverse Latino kettle in the United States. Because of history and migration, it is more Mexican- and Central American–flavored in the West and the Southwest, more Caribbean-flavored in the Northeast and the South, and a mixture of both in the Midwest. Yet the Latino communities in all of these regions are undergoing tremendous change, and the Latino populations are becoming more heterogeneous in each region. For example, the area in Miami that is known worldwide as Little

Havana is no longer predominantly Cuban; rather, Nicaraguans, Colombians, and other Latinos now constitute the majority. There are more Puerto Ricans in Florida than in New Jersey or San Juan, and they now constitute the second-largest Latino group in Florida, after Cubans. New York City now has substantial and growing Dominican, Colombian, Ecuadoran, and Mexican populations. The same is true of Los Angeles and other large cities as well as many suburban areas.

My Hopes for This Book

This book attempts to present the Latino past in motion pictures, a past that has been both glorious and problematic—but above all fascinating. It is my hope that readers will come to know many of these forgotten stars and that they will also feel a new connection to some of those with whom they may have been familiar, that they may now see them in a different light or in a different context. Perhaps having seen, through text and photos, the parade of Latino film stars from the beginning of the century to the present the reader will be able to add a strong shot of retrospective realism to the glitz and glamour of Hollywood.

It is also my hope that this book, standing as it does at the intersection of the film literature and the race and ethnicity literature, will help to fill a void in both. Film critics and researchers alike give scant voice to the presence of Latinos. Two major examples of this are the films *Salt of the Earth* and *High Noon*—both of which are classic movies that are standard components of most film studies programs. *Salt of the Earth* is often reviewed in film courses because it so exemplifies the excesses of the McCarthy era. Yet the fact that its cast is primarily Latino and that the plot is based on a real-life strike among Hispano miners in the Southwest is—at best—discussed as an incidental or tangential aspect of the film. Often, the Latino component is ignored entirely. Similarly, *High Noon* is presented in film courses because it exemplifies so well the focus on the individual in Western film and the struggle between individual heroism and group apathy in American culture. Yet attention is seldom paid to the Mexican American character played by Katy Jurado, who reflects a generally neglected part of the story of the West: the two-hundred-year history of Spanish colonial America before Anglo settlement.

The increasing numbers of Latinos in all parts of the United States has prompted a growing national awareness of the Latino presence in the United States and its antiquity, cultural richness, and expanding influence. It is my hope that this book will draw additional attention to the rich history of Latinos in the United States and to the buried Latino legacies that are part of the heritage of all the peoples of the United States, not just Latinos. It is also my hope that the book will underscore the transnational dimension of the history of Latinos in the United States, a history that has involved a continual, and often casual, crossing of hemispheric borders.

I believe that a heightened awareness of past and contemporary practices in the media can influence future policies and customs. Unfortunately, recent extensive research on the treatment of Latinos in the media continues to find that they are either invisible or relegated to minimal roles in film, print, and television. It is my hope that this book will pose questions and challenge readers to look more closely at their world and its media depictions of Latinos, as well as other groups, each of whom have had their own unique history.

The history of film is a microcosmic history of twentieth-century America, reflecting some of our best and worst moments as a nation. Scholars are just beginning to examine the influence of popular culture and mass media (in particular, film) on national identity. This book will, I hope, contribute to that reexamination. Just as it is important to look at the history of film and its role in popular culture, it is important to encourage an awareness of the history of Latinos in film as an important part of this. It is my hope that the book leads others to reexamine conventional and accepted ways of viewing our national past and to explore the stars covered here as well as others not covered. Finally, it is my hope that the book will lead people to ask deeper questions about the unique experiences of Latinos in film and popular culture.

Acknowledgments

Projects such as this, which seek to uncover what has been covered, forgotten, or manipulated for media purposes, take a huge amount of time, perseverance, and checking and rechecking. They could not be done without the assistance and support of many people along the way. I would like to acknowledge just a few who have eased the journey at particularly crucial points. The list is long and filled with wonderful people who have lightened the load immeasurably. Among those whose names are still with me are my hardworking research assistants, Katia Amaya, Arianny Nunez, Ana Orozco, Lena Rodríguez, Minerva Rodríguez Andujar, Gelvin L. Stevenson, and, in particular, Lara Pérez-Longobardo, who was involved almost from the beginning to the end; all of those in the photo posses, that is, Marta Ceballos, Marisa Ceballos, Robert Carrillo, Myra Peters-Quintero, Jessica Rodríguez, José A. Stevenson Rodríguez, Gelvina Rodríguez Stevenson, and, especially, Jimmy Rodríguez, photographer extraordinaire. The members of my initial student advisory group, Mona Butsuhara, Helen C. Hernández, Sandy Montelongo, Judazky Perez, Tino Perez, Elys Vasquez, and Valerie Yaremenko, all provided useful avenues to explore. In addition to the anonymous reviewers and those whose work has been cited in the volume, I would like to thank the following colleagues who provided invaluable comments at critical points in the journey: Al Greco, Michael Latham, Felix Matos-Rodríguez, Barbara Mundy, John Nieto-Phillips, Fath Ruffins, Chris Schmidt-Nowara, and Kirsten Swinth. I would also like to thank the staffs of the Library of Congress, the Museum of Modern Art, the New York Public Library for the Performing Arts, and the University of Southern California, in particular, Ned Comstock and Dace Taube; Caroline Sisneros, of the American Film Institute; Lauren Buisson, of the University of California at Los Angeles Special Collections Stills; Faye Thompson, Barbara Hall, and Sandra Archer, of the Margaret Herrick Library of the Academy of Motion Picture Arts and Sciences; Kristine Krueger, of the National Film Information Service; and the wonderful folks at the Smithsonian Institution Press, in particular, Scott Mahler, Emily Sollie, Robert Poarch, and Katherine Kimball. Finally, I would like to thank Fordham University for providing me with a Faculty Research Fellowship so that I could finish this work, as well as the National Museum of American History, Archives Center, for assisting me during my time there.

HEROES, LOVERS,

and Others

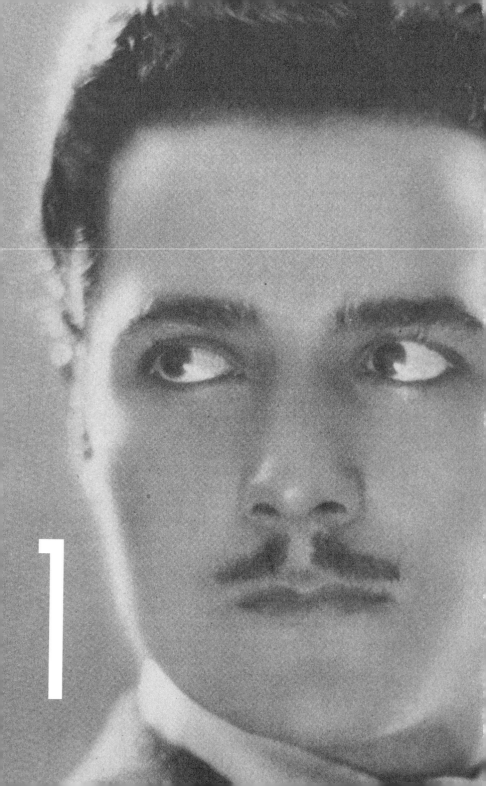

1

Hollywood and the Times

From its beginnings, Hollywood film has served as a mirror and recorder of the times. During World War II, for example, Japanese characters tended to be portrayed as demonic enemies; in the 1980s they were being presented as friendly, conservative businessmen. A simple and implicit narrative on race and ethnicity in classic Hollywood film holds that stereotypes have circulated easily and repeatedly from film to film; that ethnics and minorities have been most noticeable by their absence; that they have rarely been cast as protagonists, generally appearing as villains or dramatic foils or merely as local color or comic relief. Hollywood's relationship to each ethnic and minority group has been far more complex and nuanced, however, than this simple narrative suggests (López 1991). Each group has had its own complex history, and each group's portrayal has fluctuated with changes in consumer culture, economic prosperity, domestic and international politics, migration patterns, and the vicissitudes of power in Hollywood. Common themes flow through each of these unique group experiences, however. Issues of race, color, class, ethnicity, and gender, as well as the social currents of the times have affected the public images and private working lives of racial-ethnic film actors in all groups.

In the case of Latinos, stereotypes such as the Latin lover and his female counterpart, the Latina spitfire, have persisted throughout all eras in film. Yet unique elements have distinguished the projection of *Latinidad,* or Hispanicity, in each era. The portrayals and employment of Latino actors in Hollywood film have had a most diverse history. The early period was very likely the most generous of times for Latinos in film; many Latinos appeared in these early films, and they appealed to a wide audience. The climate warmed in the forties, when the screen image of Latinos improved, though it remained limited. The most barren of times occurred during the cold war era. The sixties and seventies were the worst of times, in terms of the quality of Latino characterizations, and the eighties represented the greatest contrast in the treatment of Latinos. The present is—relatively speaking, at least—the best of times for Latinos in film. Many more Latino characters and actors now appear in Hollywood film, though still far too few, and there are several well-known, high-profile Latino stars.

Academic and Journalistic Amnesia in Hollywood

When Hollywood films are discussed in print, a certain journalistic and academic amnesia sets in about the role of Latinos in the history of Hollywood. This has affected the way people think of both film history and the place of Latinos in that history: "What? Latinos in film? What history?" A close examination of the early history of Hollywood through the lens of the popular press of the time yields a number of surprises. A substantial number of important early Latino stars, for example, performed with distinctly discernible Spanish surnames: Myrtle Gonzalez, Beatriz Michelena, Antonio Moreno, Ramon Novarro, Dolores Del Rio, Raquel Torres, and Lupe Velez. This is in stark contrast to subsequent periods—the fifties and early sixties, for example, when the only Latino actor seen on the big screen was the occasional Latin lover, who generally did not end up winning the leading lady. There were Latino characters in films like *West Side Story* (1961) and other gang movies, but they were generally played by non-Latino actors. Often, the Latino characters in westerns were the bad guys, the nameless "banditos," or the cantina girls who had little time or substantial presence on the screen. Moreover, the characters were usually morally or esthetically limited—on the "other side," the side where few viewers wanted to be.

Television brought in Desi Arnaz (as Ricky Ricardo) and guest appearances by Carmen Miranda, as well as *The Cisco Kid* and *Zorro* series, but they were the exceptions. Although these positive characters spoke to Latinos and the rest of America, they did not speak *about* Latinos in the United States. Nor did television, film, or English-language publications generally note their relationship to a larger Spanish-speaking or Portuguese-speaking American public. Despite the presence of these "exceptional Latins," it was clear to most concerned that a Spanish surname was not an advantage—either on screen or in society. Many people tried to obscure their Spanish surnames through pronunciation ("Die as" for Díaz) or changing their names (Rodríguez to Rogers, Rivera to Rivers). In addition, most Hollywood stars hid their ethnic origins. Ethnicity was seldom talked about on television or in most movie magazines. Rather, nonethnic star names were considered more "harmonious" than ethnic names—more in "harmony," that is, with white-bread, Anglo-Saxon expectations and sounds—except, of course, for those who, like Gina Lollabrigida and Brigitte Bardot, had temporarily landed in Hollywood from another county. No, leading Hollywood stars had names like Elizabeth Taylor, John Wayne, and Grace Kelly.

It is thus surprising to discover, in examining a variety of lesser-known sources—early news clippings and books, contemporary sources on the early Hollywood period, Internet sites on silent-film stars, and popular fan magazines of the time—that in the earliest period of film, there were a considerable number of important Latino stars. The most popular fan magazine of the time, *Photoplay*, is a good barometer of the tastes of the audiences and the movie fans. Although its subscription base may have been very middle class, its actual readership was far broader. Its circulation was six times that of all the other fan magazines combined. It was also an influential player in Hollywood. Established in 1912, by the early twenties *Photoplay* had become the "queen of the fan magazines" (Fuller 1996, 150). Its influence in Hollywood was so great that Rudolf Valentino, the first and foremost Latin lover, wrote to the editor, thanking *Photoplay* for "discovering and creating" him. "You made theater managers know me," he noted, "and you caused film magazines and newspapers to be conscious of me. I am more grateful than you will ever know" (Valentino 1923, 34). Whether true or not—many people take credit for having made Valentino a star—his remarks testify to the influence and power that *Photoplay* wielded at the time in Hollywood.

In *Photoplay* issues from 1921 to 1934, numerous photos and articles feature "Latin stars" (the term used at the time), who were seen as major marquee idols. They performed alongside those who are today considered Hollywood legends, and they sometimes had top billing. They advertised popular products like Coca-Cola and Lucky Strike cigarettes. They were regularly celebrated as the ideal in beauty and physique. Perhaps most surprising, their Latin-ness was often foregrounded; moreover, consonant with the maxim that imitation is the highest form of flattery, some non-Latino stars sought to be more "Latin." They changed their names, to sound more Spanish. The men sported mustaches, and women were photographed in Spanish dress. In 1928, for example, Joan Crawford was described as "more Spanish than the Spaniards themselves" in a caption that accompanied a large photo of her in lace mantilla and a high Spanish shawl (photo caption, *Photoplay*, June 1928, 19). These were the images projected at the time; they would change dramatically in later years.

Alongside the Legends

Early Latino stars appeared with legends of the silver screen—Greta Garbo, Clara Bow, Douglas Fairbanks, Gary Cooper, and Mae West—with equal or sometimes higher billing. Furthermore, and in contrast to subsequent periods, they appeared as leads in major movies, playing diverse character roles in a variety of social positions. The well-known classic silent film *It* (1927) is a good example.

Antonio Moreno, an immigrant from Spain, began his film career in 1912. He starred in the movie *It* as the romantic lead, opposite the famous silent-screen legend, Clara Bow. Moreno was cast as neither a Latin lover nor a criminal; rather, he played Cyrus T. Waltham, a department store magnate, who has inherited the largest department store in the world. Clara Bow is Betty Lou Spence, the working-class store clerk, who falls for her boss. While working in his store, Betty Lou comes to Waltham's attention because she has that indefinable "It" quality—what would later be called sex appeal. Waltham invites her to one of his social clubs for dinner. Hastily, and with the aid of her sister (who, by the way, is an unmarried mother and, therefore, serves as the skeleton in the closet), she assembles a makeshift dress from a pair of curtains. At the club, she is seen attempting (not altogether successfully) to camouflage, or at least bridge, the social distance between herself and the other women there, who eye her as both a competitor for the attentions of this most desirable bachelor and of an "inferior" class.

After some "appropriate" (for the time) romantic play between Mr. Waltham and the "It" girl, Betty Lou invites her boss to a less stuffy outing—to Coney Island. Here, in a tumbling ride that tosses them together in hearty laughter and sheer, joyous abandonment, both characters give up any pretense of social decorum; they see themselves, and each other, for who they really are—two human beings who, despite class differences, are meant for each other. *It* is a Cinderella story of its time. (Also telling of the time, everyone in the movie—even the extras at Coney Island—is white.)

It was a blockbuster in its time, and it left its imprint on Hollywood, particularly on its speech: For years, "the 'It' girl" or "the 'It' guy" was used to describe the actor with the greatest Hollywood buzz at the moment. Film literature contains many other references to this early film and to Clara Bow's role in the film, but seldom is any reference made to Antonio Moreno, who was at the time a leading marquee idol. He had a long career in film, and though he played many Latin lovers he also played other roles and was cast in a variety of social positions.

Early Marquee Idols

Another contrast between this early period and the years that followed was the extent to which Latino actors were recognized as important stars in their day. The best evidence of this is the extraordinary amount of media attention they received. In *Photoplay*, numerous stories, photos, ads, and full-page color portrait photos featured Latin stars, along with references to them as "matinee idols" and "famous stars." They also graced the covers of many magazines. Lupe Velez, for example, appeared on the cover of no fewer than nineteen national and international magazines. To place this in context, imagine the significance of a full-page color or cover photo of a star in an issue of *People* magazine or in international magazines today. Like other major stars of the day, the private lives of these Latin stars were projected as lavish, glamorous, and rich. Ramon Novarro's extravagant lifestyle seemed to be particularly underscored. Latin stars of the day were box-office draws and were relatively well paid for their work in film. In addition to the coverage they received in the popular press, they had a great many fans. Fox Studios regularly picked up a daily load of fan letters for Dolores Del Rio from all over the world. Until recently, few Latin stars enjoyed that kind of media attention.

Advertisements

Latin stars appeared regularly in film industry advertisements. One recurring ad that ran for a number of years pictured the major MGM stars of 1929: Ramon Novarro, Greta Garbo, Lon Chaney, William Hanes, Buster Keaton, Norma Shearer, Marion Davies, and John Gilbert. A 1931 ad for the "New De Luxe Edition of the Stars of the *Photoplay*" included photos of three Latinos—Don Alvarado, Raquel Torres, and Ramon Novarro—among the twelve stars pictured. There were also full-page ads for films headlined by Latin stars: Ramon Novarro, for example, in *The Student Prince* (1928), with Norma Shearer. Again, think of the contemporary equivalents and the significance of the few stars who get full-page ads for their films. Which stars and movies receive the greatest amount of advertising? Generally, those that bring in the biggest box-office receipts.

Given the scarcity until recently of Latinos as commercial spokespeople, it is surprising to see the use of Latin stars to sell a variety of popular products, including shoes, clothes, cigarettes, face creams, hats, Coca-Cola, and household linens. From a Hollywood perspective, these ads served a dual purpose, advertising both the stars endorsing the products and their upcoming films. Two of the most interesting and somewhat amusing ads, from our present-day perspective, touted cigarettes. In the November 16, 1931, *Playbill*, Lupe Velez endorsed Lucky Strike cigarettes; the ad notes that Miss Velez was not paid for her statement, implying a "sincere" endorsement—ostensibly unrelated to the mention of her new film in the ad. In the February 13, 1938, issue of *Vogue*, Dolores Del Rio echoes similar sentiments, telling readers how gentle Luckies are on her throat. Interestingly, although the ad features Del Rio, its tag line brags that "with men who know tobacco best, it's Luckies—2 to 1." The superior credibility of men (at least with respect to cigarettes) is mentioned twice in this ad.

Best in Beauty and Physique

Hollywood has always been about beautiful faces and beautiful bodies. Present-day Latina stars frequently make the top-ten lists ranking the most beautiful, the sexiest, and so on. This is a relatively recent phenomenon, however. Consequently, it is surprising to see the extent to which Latin stars in this early period were singled out as the most beautiful, the most handsome, or those with the best bodies. In 1931 *Photoplay* named Dolores Del Rio the actress with the best figure in Hollywood—beating out such well-known stars as Greta Garbo, Carole Lombard, Joan Crawford, Clara Bow, Bebe Daniels, and Constance Bennett Fletcher. Although this was clearly far from a scientific survey (indeed, it was very likely a publicity stunt), from a more contemporary perspective the awarding of the title to a Spanish-surnamed actress was remarkable. The selection of Del Rio, according to the article, established the superiority of the roundly turned, warmly curved figure—which, it was noted, was also the figure of some of her contenders, though they received only honorable mention ("Who Has the Best Figure in Hollywood?" 1931, 34–36, 86–87).

Each year, the Western Association of Motion Picture Advertisers (WAMPA) picked thirteen promising young starlets to be "WAMPA babies." Selection as a WAMPA baby signaled a bright future in the studio system. In 1926 the association chose Dolores Del Rio, along with Joan Crawford, Mary Astor, Fay Wray, and Janet Gaynor. Lupe Velez was similarly honored two years later. In keeping with the racist standards of the times, all the WAMPA babies were white women. The only exception to this tradition was Toshia

Latino stars were often used to advertise products. Here, Latina superstar Dolores Del Rio appears in a 1938 *Vogue* magazine ad for Lucky Strikes.

Mori, an Asian American. Mori was selected in 1932 as a last-minute replacement for Lillian Miles, who failed to show up at the award ceremony (she was apparently getting married).

The significance of Latin stars—particularly women—

continued for some time. As late as 1932, *Photoplay* high-lighted Lupe Velez and Dolores Del Rio in a story about "famous faces" dining at the noted Brown Derby restaurant in Hollywood ("All the Stars Dine Here" 1932, 73–74). During the shift to talkies, the Latinas fared better than many of the Latinos. The advent of talking film favored actors whose voices or accents were deemed attractive to theatergoers. Dolores Del Rio's voice was thought to be sufficiently demure and sophisticated and to have a slightly international accent, and so she continued to play a wide variety of roles, although she played more Latin characters during the talkies era. Lupe Velez was also able to make a successful transition to sound movies in the thirties because her voice was husky and cartoon-like—a clear asset in the comedic roles she would subsequently come to play. The hands of some of these early Latin stars were immortalized in the sidewalk at Grauman's Chinese Theater in Hollywood along with other major stars in Hollywood at the time.

Latin-ness Foregrounded

The foregrounding of "Latin-ness" and Spanish or Latino origins was in keeping with a general early trend in *Photoplay* in which the origins—sometimes fabricated—of all stars were made clear. For example, *Photoplay* reported that Claudette Colbert's real name was Chauchoin and that she had been born in Paris (photo caption, *Photoplay*, January 1931, 25). Short biographies, in small print, often accompanied full-page photos of stars, giving other information such as birth date, height, weight, hair and eye color, name of spouse, and ancestral details. In the bios of "Latin" stars, even those who did not have Spanish surnames or who had changed their names to English-sounding names, their Latin American origins were accentuated. Coverage of Gilbert Roland, for example, left no doubt that he was born in Mexico.

Barry Norton (1905–56) was first introduced in a 1928 issue of *Photoplay* in a full-page photo, without reference to

The 1928 caption to this full-page photo in the largest fan magazine of the day, *Photoplay*, notes that silent-screen actor Barry Norton was born Alfredo Biraben, in Argentina.

his Latin American origins. A few months later, however, a more extensive feature article in the same magazine reported that he had been born in Buenos Aires and that his given name was Alfredo Biraben. A cute baby picture of him and a (not-so-cute) picture of his parents in Argentina were included in the article ("Doug's Office Boy Makes Good" 1929, 63, 96–97). Norton's native Argentine and upper-class origins were important features of his public image during his early years in film. (At the time, upper-class Latin American backgrounds were often underscored, and sometimes created, for many of the Latin stars.) Norton was a leading man in the silent era and appeared often in the magazine and in many Hollywood-produced English- and Spanish-language movies. However, with the advent of talkies his career declined.

Anita Page (1910–) was born Anita Pomares in New York City. Her father's family had come from El Salvador. Better known in the thirties than Barry Norton, she is also better remembered today as an important star of the silent and early talkies era—although few recall her as a Latin star. In 1929 she reportedly received more than ten thousand fan letters a week—a figure surpassed only by the reigning queen of silent film, Greta Garbo. More than one hundred fan letters came from Benito Mussolini, the Italian dictator, who wrote obsessively and several times asked for her hand in marriage. Anita Page also had a starring role in the second film ever to win an Oscar (*The Broadway Melody,* 1929). Her photo appeared often in *Photoplay,* and the magazine's coverage of her reflected an openness—albeit short lived—with regard to her Latin American origins.

Having begun in Hollywood in 1925 playing uncredited parts, Page showed up as one of three new starlets in a 1928 MGM film, *Our Dancing Daughters.* (The other two "daughters" in the film were Joan Crawford, as the redhead, and Dorothy Sebastian, as the brunette. Anita was the blonde.) A later 1928 full-page photo of her alone indicated she had just graduated from Washington Irving High School in New York and had been discovered by an arts patron (photo caption,

The 1929 caption to this photo in *Photoplay* states that "Anita Page was born Anita Pomares and she is a blond, blue-eyed Latin." She received more than ten thousand fan letters a week in 1929, second only to the reigning queen of silent film, Greta Garbo.

Photoplay, November 1928, 22). The following year, Anita appeared in a tulle-skirted flower-bedecked ballerina-type dress; the caption describes her as a "a blond, blue-eyed Latin" with "a dash of Spanish ancestry." Interestingly, despite what appears to be bobbed hair in the photo, she is also described as a new type that is superseding the boyish flapper (photo caption, *Photoplay*, August 1929, 20).

By the following year, 1930, Page's Latin American origins were foregrounded in a feature article by "Wild Mark" Busby (also known as "Don Juan"). The author jokingly describes his date with Anita, during which they were chaperoned by her family—Papa Pomares, Mrs. Pomares, and their six-year-old son, Moreno—suggesting that she came from a very strict Latin home. An accompanying illustration shows Anita playing the piano in her parents' home ("Dating Anita" 1930, 65–66, 101). The article emphasizes the extent to which Anita Page was bound by the Latin American and Spanish custom of the *chaperona*. Two more references to her later that year continue to call attention to the Latin affiliation, one noting her real name and mentioning the "Pomares tribe," the other clarifying that her father was "Spanish-French, hence the name Pomares" ("Fresh from the Camera" 1930, 19; photo caption, *Photoplay*, April 1930, 19).

After *The Broadway Melody*, in which Anita starred, won an Academy Award, references to her Latin origins disappeared. In this film, Anita played Queenie Mahoney (definitely not a Latin character), half of a singing-dancing sister act that is trying to make it on Broadway. Her character has to confront separation from her sister when she falls in love and opts for the married-with-children-and-suburban-home life over the on-the-road Broadway career. Today, though many remember her as a leading lady of Hollywood silent films, few recall her Latin connection. She retired from film in 1937, after marrying a naval officer who later taught at the University of San Diego. She raised two daughters and returned to the screen late in life and only for occasional guest appearances.

A More Latin-Sounding Name

Although it has been common practice for stars to change their names from ethnic to less ethnic, what was particularly unusual during this early period was the trend toward changing names to sound *more* Latin. Latin actors, in particular, who were born with Anglo-sounding names took on other names for their film careers to accentuate their Latin or Spanish backgrounds. The shift was openly addressed—indeed, featured—in the press at the time. For example, in 1928 *Photoplay* notes that Raquel Torres's real name was Marie Osterman and describes her as "half Mexican and half German"; the caption adds, "You can't beat that for an interesting combination" (photo caption, *Photoplay*, October 1928, 62).

In fact, Raquel Torres was born either Wilhelmina von Osterman or Paula Marie Osterman in Hermosillo, Mexico. (There are two obituaries, each giving a different birth name [Raquel Torres obituary, *Variety*, August 19, 1987; Raquel Torres obituary, *New York Times*, August 13, 1987, both in Torres clippings file]). Her father was a German mining engineer in Mexico, and her mother was apparently Mexican—although in 1933 the *New York Times* refers to her as "Spanish" (photo caption, *New York Times*, April 30, 1933, Torres clippings file). Raquel was sent to a convent school in Mexico at an early age and learned to speak both German and Spanish before she acquired English. Her mother died while Raquel was very young, and the family moved to the United States, where Raquel completed her education in a convent school in Los Angeles. Interestingly, though she came to the United States at a young age and spent most of her time here, she was commonly referred to as a "Mexican actress." Perhaps this was the other side of Latin recognition: Latinness was indelible, and one never lost it.

How much of Torres's name change was determined by her "Latin looks" and how much it reflected an attempt (hers or perhaps her studio's) to capitalize on the craze for all things

Raquel Torres, born Marie (or Wilhelmina) Osterman, starred in *White Shadows* (1928), MGM's first feature film to include fully synchronized dialogue, music, and effects. Torres is shown here in a full-page 1928 photo from *Photoplay*, the "queen of fan magazines."

Latin is not clear. It was probably a combination of both. Raquel reportedly changed her name three times "before it sounded Spanish enough to suit the movie powers that be."

According to one news report, despite her Teutonic surname, she had inherited the Latin coloring and disposition of her mother—olive complexion, black eyes, thick curly dark hair, and fiery personality—and so when opportunity knocked at her door in the form of a moving picture contract to play Spanish roles, she realized that "Billie Osterman" would never do. Adopting her mother's maiden name, she became first Hilda Torres and then, seeking a stronger connotation of "sunny Spain," Raquel Torres. Raquel made only a few films in Hollywood, where she is best remembered for having starred (at the age of nineteen) in *White Shadows* (1928), MGM's first feature film with fully synchronized dialogue, music, and effects. Torres died at the age of seventy-eight in Malibu, California, of a heart attack, having made about ten films from 1928 to 1934 ("Film Star Changed Name Three Times," *ERS*, October 21, 1931, Torres clippings file).

The case of Don Alvarado (1905–67) is similar. Born Joe Page in Amijo, New Mexico, he first appeared in *Photoplay* in 1928 with a mustache and a decidedly Latin lover quality to him. The caption to the photo further accentuates his Latin look: "As plain Joe Page, he came to Hollywood to teach dancing. The movies re-christened him Don Alvarado, as more fitting his type and his Latin ancestry. Now he is one of the most fatal of the recent discoveries" (photo caption, *Photoplay*, April 1928, 21). A few months later, in 1929, another large full-page photo of him appeared in the same magazine, but this time his mustache is gone, he is wearing a tweed jacket, and his given name is not mentioned. He could easily be Joe Page, ethnicity unknown. The caption does note his Latin ancestry, which was in "great demand" (photo caption, *Photoplay*, January 1929, 20).

Alvarado was described by one *Photoplay* reporter as "the handsomest man I have ever met" (Madeline Glass, "Spanish—with English Reserve," *Photoplay*, June 1929, Alvarado clippings file), but he did not have a major career in film. He broke into Hollywood as an extra in 1924, and toward the end of the decade he played the leading man in a few films.

Beginning as an extra in 1924, Don Alvarado, whose birth name was Joe Page, became a leading man toward the end of the decade. He is shown here in a full-page 1928 photo from *Photoplay*.